Kenya

Sean McCollum

Carolrhoda Books, Inc. / Minneapolis

Photo Acknowledgments

Photos, maps, and artworks are used courtesy of: John Erste, pp. 1, 2–3, 9, 18–19, 21, 25, 27, 35, 42; Laura Westlund, pp. 4, 29; © Phil Porter, pp. 6 (left), 19, 27, 43 (left); © Jason Laure, pp. 6 (right), 7, 13 (left and right), 14, 15 (bottom), 17, 18, 26, 28, 29 (bottom), 33 (left), 36 (top and bottom), 39 (left), 41; © Michele Burgess, pp. 8, 9 (left and right), 15 (top) 23, 25 (bottom), 30, 34, 37, 40, 43 (right); © James P. Rowan, pp. 10–11, 12, 16 (left and right), 20 (top), 29 (top), 44; UPI/Bettman, p. 11; © David F. Clobes/photo by Sue Kelm, p. 20 (bottom), 24; ©Eugene G. Schultz, pp. 22, 32; © Frank Balthis, pp. 25 (top), 38, 39 (right); © September 8th Stock, Walt/Louiseann Pietrowicz, p. 31; © Liba Taylor, p. 33. Cover photo of zebras, © Michele Burgess.

Copyright © 1999 by Sean McCollum.

All rights reserved. International copyright secured. No part of this book may be reproduced, stored in a retrieval system, or transmitted in any form or by any means—electronic, mechanical, photocopying, recording, or otherwise—without the prior written permission of Carolrhoda Books, Inc., except for the inclusion of brief quotations in an acknowledged review.

Carolrhoda Books, Inc.
c/o The Lerner Publishing Group
241 First Avenue North
Minneapolis, Minnesota 55401 U.S.A.

Website address: www.lernerbooks.com

Recipe for baked plantain adapted from *Cooking the African Way* by Constance Nabwire and Bertha Vining Montgomery (Minneapolis: Lerner Publications Company, 1988).

Words in **bold type** are explained in a glossary that begins on page 44.

Library of Congress Cataloging-in-Publication Data

McCollum, Sean.
   Kenya / by Sean McCollum.
      p.   cm. — (Globe-trotters club)
   Includes index.
   Summary: An overview of Kenya emphasizing its cultural aspects.
   ISBN 1–57505–105–2 (lib. bdg. : alk. paper)
    1. Kenya—Juvenile literature. [1. Kenya.] I. Title.
II. Series: Globe-trotters club (Series)
DT433.522.M42   1999
967.62—DC21   97–16447

Manufactured in the United States of America
1 2 3 4 5 6 – JR – 04 03 02 01 00 99

Contents

Karibuni Kenya!	5
Highs and Lows	6
Safari Central	8
Long-ago Kenyans	10
Adding to the Mix	12
Who Are You?	14
Getting Bigger	16
On the Move	18
Country Life	20
Families Matter	22
Home Sweet Home	24
Want to Learn Kiswahili?	26
Old and New Faiths	28
What's for Dinner?	30
Kenyan-style ABCs	32
Hey, Hey, a Holiday!	34
On Your Mark, Get Set	36
Singing and Swaying	38
Everyday Art	40
Tell Me a Story	42
Glossary	44
Pronunciation Guide	46
Further Reading	47
Index	48

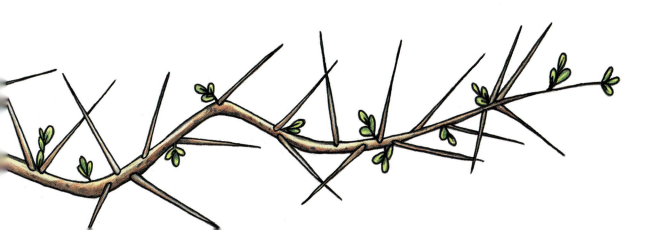

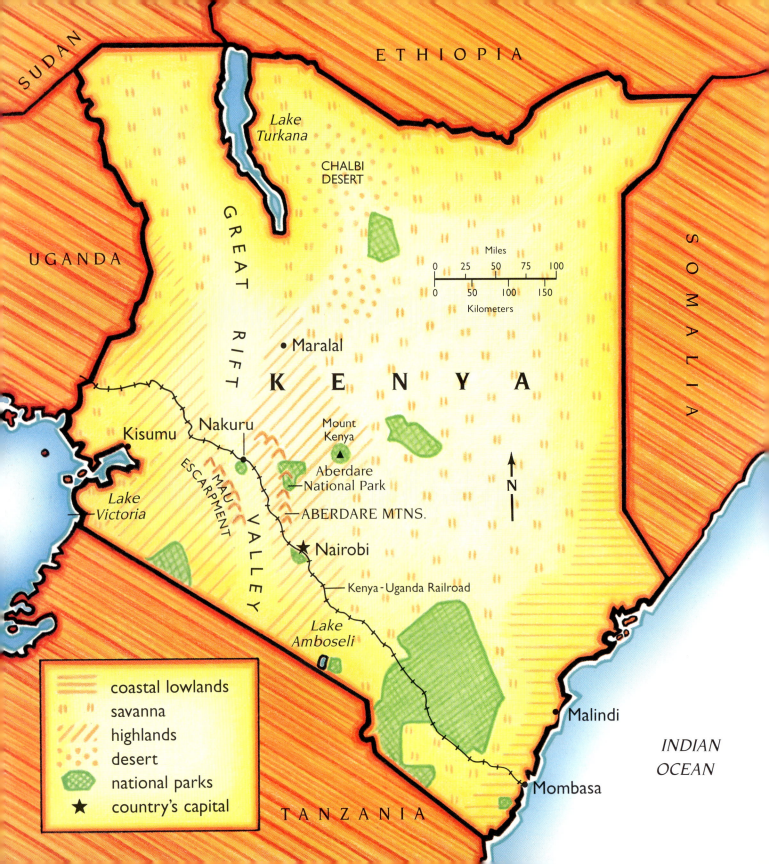

Karibuni Kenya!*

*That means "Welcome to Kenya" in Kiswahili, the national language of Kenya.

 Kenya lies on Africa's eastern coast, just below the part of the continent known as the Horn of Africa. Shaped like a rhinoceros horn, this piece of land juts into the Indian Ocean, the body of water that laps against Kenya's southeastern shore. Somalia, Kenya's neighbor to the northeast, covers much of the horn. Ethiopia stretches across most of Kenya's northern edge, with Sudan touching the rest. Uganda curls against Kenya's northwestern side, and huge Lake Victoria washes into the southwestern corner. Tanzania lies south of Kenya.

Kenya sits right on the equator—the imaginary line that divides the earth into the Northern Hemisphere and the Southern Hemisphere. This means that year-round the sun shines for 12 hours each day. Temperatures are about the same from month to month, too. What *does* change is the amount of rainfall. Kenya has two dry seasons and two wet seasons. The "short rains"—wet mornings but sunny afternoons—come in October and November. From March until June, Kenya's "long rains" fall most of the day. In the other months, Kenya dries out.

Now You See It, Now You Don't!

In the wet seasons, Lake Amboseli covers 38 square miles of Kenya's eastern **plateau.** This huge lake disappears entirely during the dry seasons. Some of Kenya's rivers do the same thing. The bodies of water often leave behind a clue—plants and trees that surround a bowl of dust. These dry holes fill up again when it rains.

The Great Rift Valley (left)—a 4,000-mile-long crack in the earth's surface—runs from the Middle East through eastern Africa. The beaches along the Indian Ocean (above) are great places to cool off in the hot, humid lowlands.

Highs and **Lows**

Traveling from east to west across southern Kenya is like climbing up and then down a wacky staircase! At Malindi, a busy city in Kenya's coastal lowlands, sandy beaches and palm trees meet the waves. Nearby Kenyan farmers grow **tropical** crops, such as coconuts, cashews, and cotton.

As you travel inland, you'll see fewer Kenyans in the **savanna,** a grassland that rises in a series of level plateaus. You may want to put on a sweater when you reach the cooler highlands, where three out of four people live.

After you climb the Aberdare Mountains, you'll come to a sudden break in Kenya's staircase—the Great Rift Valley, a steep drop that divides the highlands into eastern and western parts. Then it's up, up, up the Mau **Escarpment.** But traveling over the rest of the western highlands is mostly downhill. When you reach the bustling port city of Kisumu, change into your swimsuit for a dip in the cool waters of Lake Victoria.

Much of northern Kenya is dry and hot, especially the Chalbi **Desert**. Kenyans who live in this harsh land have good survival skills, like knowing where to dig for water during dry seasons when the lakes disappear.

Giraffes and other animals roam the open expanses of the Kenyan savanna. Few people settle in these grasslands, because rainfall isn't reliable enough to support crops.

Fast Facts about Kenya

Name: Jamhuri ya Kenya (Republic of Kenya)
Area: 224,960 square miles
Main Landforms: Aberdare Mountains, Mau Escarpment, Great Rift Valley, Chalbi Desert
Highest Point: Mount Kenya (17,058 feet)
Lowest Point: Sea level
Animals: Antelopes, baboons, cheetahs, elephants, giraffes, hyenas, jackals, leopards, lions, rhinoceroses
Capital City: Nairobi
Other Major Cities: Mombasa, Kisumu, Nakuru, Malindi
Languages: English (official), Kiswahili (national)
Money Unit: Kenya shilling

Safari **Central**

Grab your camera and slather on the sunscreen—we're going on a safari! You'll make new friends from around the world who've traveled to Kenya just to see and photograph the animals.

As the safari truck bounces over the savanna, you might feel like you're in a zoo without cages. Yikes! The African lion, the so-called king of the jungle, really prefers the grassy plains. Lionesses (females) do the hunting, bounding after zebras, wildebeests, and many types of antelopes. Graceful leopards hunt alone, stashing leftovers in trees. Speed demon of the animal world, the cheetah races up to 60 miles per hour. Did you hear something rustling through the tall grass? It could be an African elephant, a giraffe, or a rhinoceros.

A lioness and her cubs relax in the savanna. Chasing after food takes lots of energy, but these hunters recover by spending up to 20 hours a day catnapping.

In the past, trophy hunters took home the heads or hides of these amazing creatures. Because of hunting and the growing numbers of Kenyans who spread over much of the animals' **range,** the nation's wildlife population plunged. To protect animals from becoming extinct, the Kenyan government set up **wildlife refuges.**

A Baboon Stole My Camera!

Does this sound a lot like "My dog ate my homework"? Well, at a hotel called the Treetops in Kenya's Aberdare National Park, theft by baboons is not a one-time occurrence. Baboons, along with other wildlife, are drawn to the waterhole close to the hotel. From the dining-room windows, guests can watch animals come from the bush to drink or bathe. Meanwhile, baboons sneak into open guest-room windows—and out again, armed with cameras and whatever else catches their fancy.

Kenya's wildlife is the nation's greatest tourist attraction. Many visitors come to Kenya to see elephants (left), **giraffes** (below), and other animals while on a safari.

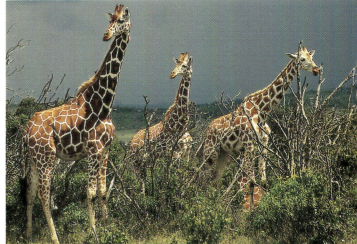

Long-ago Kenyans

 When you hear a family speaking a foreign language, what's the first question that pops into your head? Many people want to know from which part of the world the family traveled. That question has helped linguists (people who study languages) figure out how the roughly 40 **ethnic groups** that reside in Kenya came to live there.

People within an ethnic group share a religion, a history, and a language. This means that in Kenya dozens of languages are spoken. But linguists have found that many of these languages are related. In fact, because of similarities between languages, they've linked modern-day Kenyans to three branches of ancient peoples.

Around 3,000 years ago, Africans from other parts of the continent began to migrate to what would become Kenya and pushed out the groups that were already there. These days about half of Kenyans can trace their roots to West African groups who spoke Bantu languages. Moving east over many centuries, these farming peoples looked for fertile land and settled to the north of Lake Victoria, on the southern coast, and in central Kenya.

Fertile farmland was one of the reasons why many different ethnic groups came to Kenya from western, northern, and northeastern Africa.

Meanwhile, Nilotic peoples—from the area near the Nile River that's become present-day Sudan—headed south and imported their own group of languages to Kenya. Nilotic groups settled in the Great Rift Valley and near Lake Victoria. The **nomadic** Cushitic peoples, whose **descendants** live mostly in the dry grasslands of northern and northeastern Kenya, brought languages from modern-day Ethiopia and Somalia.

Digging for Answers

In the mid-1900s, Louis and Mary Leakey *(below)*, a famous scientific team, discovered ancient **fossilized** skulls when they dug up soil in parts of the Great Rift Valley. Some scientists think that these and other skeletons found in the valley are from our earliest **ancestors**. So the Great Rift Valley is often called the "cradle of humanity."

The Leakeys' son Richard and his group dug near Lake Turkana in northern Kenya. In 1984 Kamoya Kimeu, a Kenyan scientist on Richard's team, unearthed an almost complete skeleton. Experts think these bones date back 1.6 million years. And you thought your parents grew up in the olden days!

Adding to the Mix

 Nearly 99 percent of Kenyans have African ancestry. But Middle Easterners, Europeans, and Asians have contributed to Kenya's ethnic makeup and culture. Seafaring Arab and Persian traders from the Middle East visited the shores of East Africa about 2,000 years ago. By the A.D. 700s, Arabs had built coastal cities in what would become Kenya. By the 1500s, the Portuguese had control of the Kenyan coast, but Arabs had regained their authority by the late 1600s.

Europeans grew more interested in Africa for its minerals and farmland during the 1800s. Great Britain conquered East Africa in 1895 and divided it into **colonies**—one of which is present-day Kenya. The British set up plantations (large

Fort Jesus, located in Mombasa, is a reminder of the Portuguese occupation of the Kenyan coast. The Portuguese used the area as a trading base for almost 200 years.

farms) and ranches in Kenya's fertile highlands, displacing many of the local farmers. Putting their language and systems of government and education into place, the British built cities, roads, and railroads. They imported workers from India, which at that time was another part of the British Empire, to help lay the tracks. After the railroad was completed, many Indians stayed, becoming successful merchants.

A lot of Kenyans resented British rule. In 1963, after a long push for independence, Kenya became a free nation. Some British left Kenya, but others stayed to help build the new country.

Modern-day *dhows* **(left) along the Kenyan coast reflect the Arab influence on Kenyan culture. These sailboats were first used by long-ago Arab traders. Asian Kenyans (above) are descendants of workers the British imported from India.**

This woman is a member of the Kikuyu, the largest ethnic group in Kenya.

Who Are **You?**

 Listen to two Kenyans introduce themselves. "I'm Paul Odinga of the Luo." "I'm Julie Thuku. I'm Kikuyu." They are telling one another their names and their ethnic backgrounds.

More than one out of five Kenyans is Kikuyu, the nation's largest ethnic group. A Bantu-speaking people, many Kikuyu are highland farmers. Some city-dwelling Kikuyu hold jobs in government and international business. Other Bantu-speakers are the Luhya, the Kamba, the Meru, and the Swahilis.

The Luo, the largest group of non-Bantu-speaking people in Kenya, have Nilotic roots. The Luo living close to Lake Victoria are expert fishers, but many Luo also work in Kenyan cities. The Nilotic Kalenjin became farmers in the Great Rift Valley. Fewer in number, the Nilotic Turkana herd and fish near Lake Turkana in northwestern Kenya. The nomadic Masai and Samburu, also Nilotic peoples, move in search of grass and water for their animals.

One or Many?

The British decided that Kenya should be a political region distinct from the rest of East Africa. Until that time, the ethnic groups that resided in the colony hadn't thought of themselves as connected. These days Kenya's leaders want citizens to view themselves as Kenyans. *Harambee,* the government's goal, means "all pull together" in Kiswahili, the national language. But Kenya's ethnic groups often compete for resources, and many Kenyans want to keep ties with their age-old way of life.

This Samburu boy (above) **comes from an ethnic group that maintains a nomadic lifestyle. Many Luo** (below) **fish the waters of Lake Victoria in southwestern Kenya for their livelihood.**

Cushitic peoples—including the Somali, Boran, Gabbra, Galla, El Molo, and Boni—still herd in Kenya's dry northern regions, just as their ancestors did. In years when rainfall is very low, Cushitic herders and their animals have a hard time getting enough to eat.

Getting **Bigger**

Nairobi, Kenya's capital, is also the nation's biggest city. About 1 out of 15 Kenyans lives in the capital. That's a lot of people! Nairobi is the place to do business in East Africa. High-rise buildings tower above busy sidewalks. People from all of Kenya's ethnic groups live in the city or come to the capital to sell their goods. Some Kenyans—especially the Kikuyu and the Luo—have worked hard to learn business skills, which bring high-paying jobs.

Because the city has electricity, people in Nairobi tend to stretch out their evenings longer than their relatives in the villages do. After the workday ends, city folks may head out for a night on the town. Some people grab a bite to eat at a restaurant and then go to a movie. Folks with lots of energy meet friends at a local club and dance away the hours.

Architecture in Nairobi reflects Kenya's cultural history. The National Archives (left) **is one of many buildings in Nairobi that the British built. The designers of the Kenyatta International Conference Center** (above) **blended traditional African styles with modern architecture.**

Many young Kenyans who come to Nairobi end up living in shantytowns.

Population Boom

Kenya has one of the fastest-growing populations in the world. Unless people have fewer children, the population will double in 27 years. That means fitting 29 million more people into the same amount of space, and Kenyans are already facing a land shortage.

Many young adults who want to farm or herd can't get land and must move to the city, especially Nairobi, to find work. Newcomers with little formal education often find only low-paying jobs. And builders in Nairobi can't keep up with the numbers of people that arrive. As a result, shantytowns, where people construct homes from scrap metal and cardboard, have sprung up on Nairobi's outskirts.

On the Move

Tourist-filled jumbo jets from all over the world fly into Nairobi's international airport. But you'll see few cars on Kenya's roads. People often rely on public buses and trains. And many Kenyans think nothing of walking miles.

Kenyans also ride in private vans called *matatus*. Pile in if you don't mind getting squished. Cheap fares attract lots of riders. Drivers going to the same place compete for customers. If Kenyans have a choice, they often climb aboard the matatu that's most crowded. That's because drivers will leave only when they've stacked people on top of other riders' laps and filled any remaining space with packages and maybe a chicken or two.

All aboard! Kenyans crowd into a matatu in Nairobi. The ride may be very bumpy, because only about 15 percent of the nation's roads are paved. During the rainy seasons, travel over unpaved roads is often impossible.

If you need to get somewhere on time or if crazy driving makes you queasy, don't take a matatu. After the long delay in starting a journey, drivers try to make up lost time. They soar over Kenya's unpaved roads, kicking up clouds of dust. Hang on!

On Track

One of Africa's best railways runs between Uganda and the Kenyan port city of Mombasa. Inland farmers transport their tea, coffee, and produce to the coast by train. From Mombasa ships carry Kenyan goods to other countries. For the return trip, workers load up the freight cars with imported computers and cars.

Many of Kenya's

In this Kikuyu farming village (left), **the small houses are made of branches and thatched grass. A Kenyan woman** (below) **carries a load of sweet potatoes on her head.**

Country Life

Do you know anyone who lives on a farm? Most Kenyans make their living in agriculture. Small farming villages dot Kenya's fertile highlands. During the day grown-ups and kids keep busy. Children help their moms plant, care for, and harvest the fields by hand. Usually the family *shamba* (farm) is small, producing enough food to feed the family.

If the crops do well, women take the extra grain, beans, fruits, and veggies to the village's open-air market, where vendors sell cloth and other handmade goods. After

farming peoples hold festivities to celebrate harvesttime.

setting up shop, women chat to catch up on what's been happening. Many men work on plantations that grow coffee and tea, Kenya's two largest cash crops.

Kids aren't finished with their chores when they're done in the fields. Most of the older children baby-sit their younger brothers and sisters. They also help cook meals, wash clothes, and carry water from the well. More country kids go to school than ever before.

After a long day, kids get together to play games. Men talk over coffee or tea. Women may entertain fellow villagers with stories. But when the sun goes down, many Kenyans hit the sack because lots of villages don't have electricity.

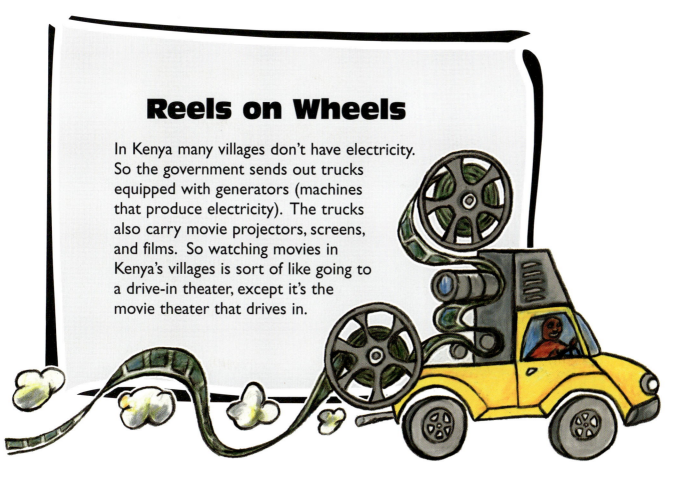

Reels on Wheels

In Kenya many villages don't have electricity. So the government sends out trucks equipped with generators (machines that produce electricity). The trucks also carry movie projectors, screens, and films. So watching movies in Kenya's villages is sort of like going to a drive-in theater, except it's the movie theater that drives in.

Families **Matter**

Kenyans keep close ties with their families. And when Kenyans talk about families, they mean aunts, uncles, cousins, and grandparents, too. Several generations often live in the same village. If young adults move to the city for work, they come home to be part of holidays and important family occasions, such as weddings and funerals.

Most kids in Kenya come from big families with more than five

All in the Family

Here are the Kiswahili words for family members. Practice using these terms on your own family. See if they can understand you!

grandfather	*babu*	(BAH-boo)
grandmother	*nyanya*	(NYAH-nyah)
father	*baba*	(BAH-bah)
mother	*mama*	(MAH-mah)
uncle	*mjomba*	(mm-JOHM-bah)
aunt	*mbiomba*	(mm-bee-OHM-bah)
son	*bin*	(BEEN)
daughter	*binti*	(BEEN-tee)
brother	*ndugu*	(nn-DOO-goo)
sister	*dada*	(DAH-dah)

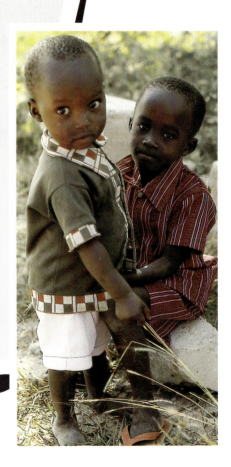

Almost half of Kenya's population is under 15 years old. That means Kenyan villages have lots of children. Many village kids are related.

brothers and sisters. And children may have many half brothers and half sisters, too. Kenyan tradition allows a man to have as many wives as he can afford. Nineteenth-century Christian missionaries discouraged this practice, which is known as **polygyny.** Even so, these days it's not uncommon for Kenyan men—including those who have adopted Christianity—to have more than one wife.

Home Sweet Home

Some Kenyan city dwellers and villagers live in modern houses or apartments with plumbing and electricity. These homes may have metal or shingled roofs, concrete floors, and windows. People sometimes use stones or bricks for walls.

In many villages, however, people follow the age-old housing customs of their ethnic group. Tradition determines the shape and style of the house and who lives in it. Sometimes a husband lives with his wife and children. But in other ethnic groups, a man lives alone. Each of his wives has a separate house where she lives with her children. Women and children of yet another group will sleep in one area of the house, while the men spread their sleeping mats in another.

Villagers build their homes with materials they collect nearby. Many rural peoples make the frame from branches and then plaster the walls with a mixture of grass and clay or mud. A roof thatched from palm leaves or grass keeps the house

Kenyans build houses in different shapes and sizes and from many different materials. Some Kenyan farmhouses (left) **consist of branches, logs, and mud, while many homes in Nairobi** (facing page, top) **are made of brick. This Masai woman** (facing page, bottom) **is fixing the roof of her home.**

Sidetrack

Does your mom or dad ever complain that you're wasting water if you leave the faucet dripping? Kenyan kids and women must carry heavy containers from wells—sometimes for several miles—or hire someone to deliver jugs of water. So Kenyan kids don't take water for granted.

snug during the rainy seasons. Standing up straight is impossible for adults in some styles of Kenyan homes because the ceilings are typically just five feet high!

These advertisements at a Nairobi train station are in English, Kenya's official language.

Want to Learn **Kiswahili?**

Hakuna matata! That means "no problem" in Kiswahili, one of the most widely used languages in Kenya. Each of Kenya's many ethnic groups also has its own language. In villages or when city families are at home, people use the language of their ethnic group.

But more and more Kenyans are learning Kiswahili—the national language—so they can understand one another when they meet in the market, at school, or at work. And when Kenyan kids grow up, those who know Kiswahili and English will have an easier time finding jobs.

English—the official language—became important in Kenya during colonial rule. It's the language used in government and international business. Kenyan kids who go to high school study English.

Did you see the movie The Lion King?

Did you happen to wonder why the lion was named Simba?

In Kiswhaili simba *means "lion."*

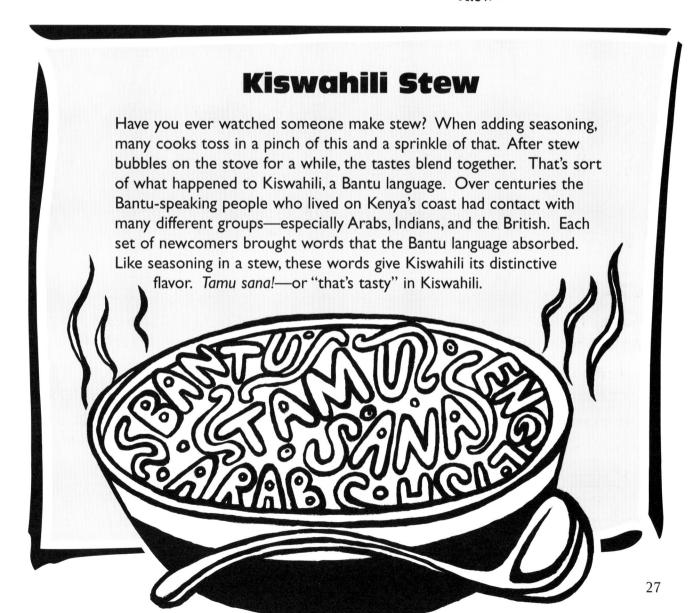

Kiswahili Stew

Have you ever watched someone make stew? When adding seasoning, many cooks toss in a pinch of this and a sprinkle of that. After stew bubbles on the stove for a while, the tastes blend together. That's sort of what happened to Kiswahili, a Bantu language. Over centuries the Bantu-speaking people who lived on Kenya's coast had contact with many different groups—especially Arabs, Indians, and the British. Each set of newcomers brought words that the Bantu language absorbed. Like seasoning in a stew, these words give Kiswahili its distinctive flavor. *Tamu sana!*—or "that's tasty" in Kiswahili.

Old and New Faiths

A Kenyan couple (above) **is married in a Christian wedding ceremony. Mosques** (facing page, top) **are places of worship for Kenya's Muslims.**

More than half of all Kenyans are Christians. Protestant and Catholic churches both have large numbers of followers. During the mid-1800s, European missionaries introduced Christianity to people living in what became Kenya.

About one-fourth of Kenyans, especially those who are herders, prefer to keep their age-old belief systems. These traditional religions teach that spirits live within rocks, trees, and animals. Acknowledging these spirits is important. That's why some Kenyans will apologize to an animal before killing it. Another traditional belief is that ancestors have spiritual power. In times of trouble or on happy occasions, a Kenyan may pray to a relative who has died, asking for guidance or a blessing. Many Kenyans blend their traditional beliefs with Christianity.

About 5 percent of Kenyans are Muslims, or followers of the Islamic religion. When Indians came to work on the railroad, they brought Hinduism, a religion widely practiced in India.

Dear Grandma and Grandpa,
Mombasa is cool, even though it's hot! We sailed from the island city into the Indian Ocean on a dhow (boat). Mombasa is East Africa's main port so we saw tons of huge ships. Long-ago Arab traders stayed here and at other places on the coast. They created a brand new culture called Swahili with the local Bantu-speaking people. From the dhow, we saw mosques—places where some Swahilis worship. The roofs have domes that look kind of like onions.
                                    See you soon!

The Diviner

If a villager experiences illness or bad luck, the person may ask the village diviner for help. The diviner chooses the appropriate treatment, which may be to give the individual a charmed necklace, medicinal herbs, or advice. By casting a spell to block the hex, the diviner can also help someone who believes he or she has been cursed by a witch.

Some ethnic groups in Kenya consider it rude to eat inside.

What's for Dinner?

If you ask Kenyan kids, "What's for dinner?" a lot of them will answer *ugali*. Ugali is usually cornmeal and water or milk cooked into a doughy porridge. But sometimes Kenyans make ugali from ground millet or cassava. Vegetables, such as spinach, may accompany the porridge. Irio—mashed corn, potatoes, beans, and peas—is also a popular meal.

Many Kenyans eat what they grow on their shamba. Besides the ingredients for ugali and irio, farmers frequently plant wheat, rice, sweet potatoes, and green vegetables. Fruit—especially mangoes, papayas, pineapples, and plantains (a type of banana)—plays a big role in Kenyan meals. Cooks prepare plantains in many ways—baked, grilled, fried, and steamed. One Kenyan standby is *matoke*, mashed plantains.

Many Kenyans grow the ingredients for dishes such as irio on their own farms.

If they have meals outdoors, they can invite passersby to join them!

People who live near water often eat fish. On the coast, fish covered with spicy coconut sauce is a favorite. Most Kenyans, even those ethnic groups who herd animals, don't eat a lot of meat. This doesn't mean that herders don't depend on their cattle or goats for nourishment. They eat a yogurtlike mixture of milk and blood, which they withdraw from the animal's neck without harming it.

Baked Plantain on the Shell

Kenyans prepare plantain in many ways. If you lived in Kenya's highlands, you'd probably head outside to pick sun-ripened plantains just before you baked them. This recipe serves four people.

You will need:
4 large, ripe plantains
1/2 cup brown sugar
3/4 teaspoon cinnamon
1/4 cup butter or margarine, melted

1. Preheat oven to 350°F.
2. Wash plantains and cut in half lengthwise. Do not peel.
3. Arrange plantains in a shallow baking dish with cut sides facing up.
4. In a small bowl, combine brown sugar, cinnamon, and melted butter. Stir well.
5. Pour brown sugar mixture over the plantains.
6. Cover dish and bake for 35 minutes or until plantains are soft.
7. Remove from oven and let cool slightly before serving.

Kenyan-style ABCs

Most Kenyan kids go to elementary school, which lasts for eight years. The government doesn't require that parents send their children to school. But grown-ups know that a good education will help their kids to find jobs in Kenya's quickly changing society.

Most children begin school when they are six years old. In areas with government-run schools, parents pay only for uniforms and books. Poorer families work hard to save for these expenses. Most schools run all year, but students get vacations during March, July, and November. Youngsters study Kiswahili, math, geography, science, and agriculture.

Since 1963, when the nation became independent, Kenya's government has built many new schools and improved the educational system. High school students (left) **and graduates of the University of Nairobi** (facing page, top) **hope they'll be able to find good jobs.**

Many teenagers set off to work after finishing elementary school. If parents want their kids to attend high school, the family must pay tuition and other educational expenses. Often parents can't afford to educate all their children, so they send the oldest. After the first child graduates and begins work, he or she helps pay the way for younger family members. But before kids are accepted into high school, they must pass a tough test.

A Girl from the Coast

Meet 11-year-old Salaama Katama, who lives in Magogoni, a town on Kenya's coast. Salaama goes to an elementary school in nearby Mombasa. She studies hard so she'll get into a good high school. Salaama is excited to begin English classes and has already picked up a few phrases.

The Uhuru Monument in Nairobi (left) honors Kenya's fight for independence. Kenya's leaders chose the colors for the nation's flag (below) carefully. Black stands for Kenya's people, red represents their struggle for freedom, and green reflects the importance of agriculture. Two white stripes symbolize peace and unity. Placed in the middle of the flag, a shield and two crossed spears show Kenyans' commitment to freedom.

Hey, Hey, a Holiday!

On December 12, 1963, Kenyans gathered for a ceremony in Nairobi. The crowd looked up at the British flag. Then the lights went out. When they flickered back on, Kenya's flag waved. People greeted the change in national leadership with cries of *uhuru*, or "freedom" in Kiswahili.

Each year people remember Kenya's Independence Day. Many people travel to their home villages to spend the day with relatives. Those who stay in the cities enjoy the huge parades that wind down the streets. Traditional dancers and musicians, often dressed in elaborate costumes, perform for the crowds. In Nairobi soldiers march past the platform from which Kenya's president gives a speech. Paratroopers' white parachutes fill the sky.

Religious holidays are also important to Kenyans. Christmas and Easter mean the most to the country's Christians. After Muslim kids have reached adolescence, they join the grown-ups in the month-long Ramadan activities. During this month, Muslims fast (don't eat or drink) from dawn until sunset, when they eat a light meal before evening prayers. Muslims celebrate the end of Ramadan with a three-day festival called Id al-Fitr.

Camel Back, Anyone?

Are you ready for a crazy day? The Maralal International Camel Derby may be just the ticket. Every October camel racers of all skill levels gather in this highland town to ride the ornery animals. Have you heard the expression "spitting mad"? These stubborn creatures may spit or kneel down when racers want them to go.

Kenyan runners (left) **excel at the steeplechase, a long-distance race that involves jumping over hurdles. Kenyans of all ages enjoy watching and playing soccer** (below).

On Your Mark, Get Set

Go! In 1996 Kenyan runners took the first five places in the world-famous Boston Marathon (26.2-mile race). Kenya's long-distance runners have won international fame in other arenas, too. Team Kenya won eight medals in the 1996 Summer Olympics.

Football, called soccer in the United States, is the favorite team sport of most Kenyans. Nearly every village sets aside a playing field. The goal posts are sometimes just sticks, and the ball may be bundled-up rags. But the athletes' clever moves always make the games exciting. British settlers introduced cricket and rugby, as well as golf and tennis, which have gained some popularity in Kenya.

When Kenyan kids aren't racing across a stretch of savanna or kicking a soccer ball, they try to beat one another in a board game called *kigogo*.

Have Fun!

Try making your own kigogo board, and then follow the rules listed below. This is just one of the many versions of kigogo that Kenyans play.

You will need:
- 2 empty egg cartons • transparent tape • scissors
- 48 markers—use dried beans, small pebbles, or marbles

Make the Board
1. Cut 2 egg cups from one of the egg cartons. Discard cut carton.
2. With the tape, attach 1 egg cup to each end of the whole carton.

Play the Game
1. Place the board between 2 players so that the end cups are to the right and left. Players own the 6 cups nearest them and the end cup to their right. Players store any markers they win in this end cup. Put 4 markers in each of the middle 12 cups.

2. The youngest player starts by picking up all the markers from any one of her cups. The player works toward her end cup, dropping 1 marker into each cup along the way.
   - If she drops the last marker of her turn in her own end cup, she gets to go again, picking up all the markers from any of her other cups.
   - If she has more markers left to drop after putting one in her end cup, she drops them one at a time into cups on her opponent's side of the board, beginning with the cup next to her end cup and working to the left. (She may even have to drop a marker in her opponent's end cup, which he then gets to keep.)

3. Players take turns, repeating step 2.
   - If a player drops the last marker of their turn in one of their own empty cups, the player wins all of the markers in the cup next door on their opponent's side. Players keep their winnings in their own end cup.

4. The game is over when one of the players has markers in only their end cup. The player with the most markers in their end cup is the winner.

These Samburu men are participating in a special dance. They leap straight up in the air and shimmy their shoulders before they come down. The Samburu will often perform this dance for tourists.

When performing traditional dances,

Singing and Swaying

How do people celebrate in Kenya? You guessed it—by making or moving to music! Ethnic groups have passed down traditional dances for special occasions.

Long-ago Kenyans composed music to go along with the dances. The birth of a child, the passage of girls and boys into adulthood, marriages, and funerals all call for dancing. Kenyans traditionally danced to contact spiritual powers. But young men sometimes dance for another reason—to impress their girlfriends.

Kids often perform songs or dances at holiday events. A popular type of song is known as "call and response." A schoolgirl may begin to sing in a high, clear voice. Others girls, forming a half circle, sing in response to her as they sway and clap

Kenyans may put on elaborate costumes, including headdresses.

in time. One feature common to much Kenyan music is that it's polyrhythmic. This means that the instruments or voices go at different beats on purpose.

In the cities, young adults like to go to nightclubs to hear the latest sounds. Musicians constantly mix the old and new. One band member might strum an electric guitar while another musician beats a hand-carved wooden drum like those played long ago. Kenyan bands also bring together American rock and roll or big-band music with African rhythms for a brand-new sound. If songwriters want most Kenyans to understand the words, they write them in Kiswahili or English.

Music is a big part of Kenyan life. Youngsters perform at music competitions in Nairobi (left), **while street musicians** (above) **play songs on old guitars and homemade instruments.**

Everyday Art

Kenyans take pride in making beautiful everyday objects. Some groups create colorful textiles by using a method called batik. The craftsperson carefully draws a design on cotton cloth with melted wax and then dips the cloth into dye. The dye doesn't seep in where the wax is. Besides the shapes the artist creates on purpose, tiny cracks in the wax form other interesting patterns.

Girls and women in Kenya enjoy making colorful jewelry. The Samburu and Masai peoples are known for their impressive beadwork. Kenyan jewelry can tell a lot about the person who wears it. The number of necklaces a woman wears may reveal whether she's married, if she has children, and might also tell the extent of her husband's wealth.

Carving has long been part of Kenyan tradition. The Kamba from the southern savanna transform ebony—a dark hardwood that grows in northeastern Kenya—into intricate drums, dance masks, and gleaming statues of humans and animals. The Kisii of southwestern Kenya carve Kisii stone, a soft, smooth rock. It comes in a variety of colors, including light pink.

Kenyans still use some of the beautiful objects they create. But craftspeople sell much of their work to tourists at bustling open-air markets or stores. Art dealers purchase Kenyan crafts to sell in other parts of the world.

The Masai people string beads together to create colorful necklaces (facing page) **and other types of jewelry. This Kamba artist** (right) **is putting the finishing touches on an ebony sculpture.**

Tell Me a Story

In the past, Kenyans didn't have written literature—they listened to stories. Kenyans verbally passed down the history and beliefs of their ethnic group. Musicians traditionally played flutes while the storyteller spun a tale.

Even these days, when many Kenyan kids can read, they love hearing a storyteller call out *Sikilizeni hadithi yangu*, which is Kiswahili for "listen to my story." In villages children and grown-ups will often gather around a storyteller. Many

Check It Out

Did you know that the character of Bre'r Rabbit originated in Africa? This clever critter always comes out on top because he plays tricks on the other animals. Beginning in the 1600s, Africans were captured and shipped to North America as slaves. They were able to bring little else with them but age-old stories. In the United States, the rabbit took on its American name. But in Kenya the rabbit has names in many languages, including a nickname that means "the one that sleeps while his eyes are open."

Some Kenyans play bamboo flutes (left) and other instruments to accompany storytellers as they weave their tales. Animals, such as the leopard (below), play a prominent role in many Kenyan stories.

Kenyan tales are about animals, and the storyteller creates a special voice for each one and acts out the plot—almost like a play. Some stories are ancient, but every telling is a bit different. Find a comfortable place to sit because storytellers sometimes go on for hours!

The country of Kenya is named after Mount Kenya, the second-highest point in Africa. In the Kikuyu language Kenya means "mountain of brightness." The Kikuyu, who settled near the mountain and for whom it's sacred, build their houses with the door facing the peak.

Glossary

ancestor: A long-ago relative, such as a great-grandparent.

colony: A territory ruled by a country that is located far away.

descendant: A person who came from an earlier person, family, or ethnic group. An individual descends directly from his or her parents, but a person's family tree can be traced to larger groups of long-ago relatives.

desert: A dry, sandy region that receives low amounts of rainfall.

escarpment: A cliff that is steep and high.

ethnic group: A large community of people that shares a number of social features in common, such as language, religion, or customs.

fossilized: When remains, such as leaves or bones, of long-ago plants or animals have hardened or have left prints on rocks or in bogs.

nomadic: A way of life that involves moving from place to place in search of food, water, or pasture.

plateau: A large area of high, level land.

polygyny: The practice of a man having more than one wife at the same time.

range: The region in which an animal or plant naturally occurs.

savanna: A tropical grassland where annual rainfall varies from season to season.

tropical: Of or relating to the tropics, which is the hot, wet zone around the earth's equator between the Tropic of Cancer and the Tropic of Capricorn.

wildlife refuge: Land set aside as a safe place for wild animals to live. On refuges, where the animals' natural surroundings are preserved, laws prevent unauthorized hunting.

While in Kenya

- Do call older men *mzee*, which means "respected elder."
- Do shake hands. To show respect to adults, grasp your right wrist with your left hand as you shake.
- Don't signal "come here" by curling your index finger. In Kenya this is a rude gesture. Kenyans indicate they want someone to come close by holding out a hand palm down and waving the fingers.
- Don't say "I'm full" after eating a big meal. In Kenya this means that you're going to have a baby.

Pronunciation Guide

Aberdare	ab-uhr-DAR
hakuna matata	hah-KOO-nah mah-TAH-tah
harambee	hah-RAHM-bay
irio	ee-REE-oh
Jamhuri ya Kenya	jahm-HOO-ree yah KEHN-yuh
Kamba	KAHM-bah
karibuni	kah-ree-BOO-nee
kigogo	kee-GOH-goh
Kikuyu	kee-KOO-yoo
Kisumu	kee-SOO-moo
Kiswahili	kee-swah-HEE-lee
Luhya	LOO-ya
Luo	LOO-oh
Masai	MAH-sy
matatu	mah-TAH-too
matoke	mah-TOH-kay
Mau Escarpment	MOW ehs-CAHRP-mehnt
Mombasa	mohm-BAH-sah
mzee	MM-zay
Nairobi	ny-ROH-bee
polygyny	puh-LIH-juh-nee
Ramadan	RAH-muh-dahn
Salaama Katama	sah-LAH-mah kah-TAH-mah
shamba	SHAHM-bah
sikilizeni hadithi yangu	see-kee-lee-ZAY-nee haw-DEE-thee YAHNG-goo
Somali	soh-MAH-lee
tamu sana	TAH-moo SAH-nah
Turkana	tuhr-KAN-uh
ugali	oo-GAH-lee
uhuru	oo-HOO-roo

Further Reading

Buettner, Dan. *Africatrek: A Journey by Bicycle through Africa*. Minneapolis: Lerner Publications Company, 1997.

Finley, Carol. *The Art of African Masks*. Minneapolis: Lerner Publications Company, 1998.

Kenya in Pictures. Minneapolis: Lerner Publications Company, 1997.

King, Bridget A. C., ed. *Beneath the Rainbow: A Collection of Children's Stories and Poems from Kenya*. Nairobi: Jacaranda Designs, 1992.

MacMillan, Dianne M. *Cheetahs*. Minneapolis: Carolrhoda Books, Inc., 1997.

McNeil, Heather. *Hyena and the Moon: Stories to Tell from Kenya*. Englewood, CO: Libraries Unlimited, 1994.

Nabwire, Constance and Bertha Vining Montgomery. *Cooking the African Way*. Minneapolis: Lerner Publications Company, 1988.

Pateman, Robert. *Kenya*. North Bellmore, NY: Marshall Cavendish, 1993.

Silver, Donald M. *African Savanna*. New York: Scientific American Books for Young Readers, 1994.

Temko, Florence. *Traditional Crafts from Africa*. Minneapolis: Lerner Publications Company, 1996.

Walker, Sally M. *Rhinos*. Minneapolis: Carolrhoda Books, Inc., 1996.

Metric Conversion Chart

WHEN YOU KNOW:	MULTIPLY BY:	TO FIND:
teaspoon	5.0	milliliters
Tablespoon	15.0	milliliters
cup	0.24	liters
inches	2.54	centimeters
feet	0.3048	meters
miles	1.609	kilometers
square miles	2.59	square kilometers
degrees Fahrenheit	5/9 (after subtracting 32)	degrees Celsius

Index

animals, 7, 8–9, 43
Arabs, 12
art, 40–41

Bantu-speaking peoples, 10, 14, 27
British, 12–13, 15, 16

cities, 6, 7, 14, 16–17
colonies, 12, 15, 26
Cushitic peoples, 11, 15

dancing, 38–39
deserts, 7

electricity, 16, 21, 24
equator, 5
ethnic groups, 10–11, 12, 14–15, 16, 24, 26

families, 22–23
farmers, 6, 11, 12–13, 14, 19, 20–21, 30
food, 27, 30–31

government, 15, 32
Great Rift Valley, 6, 11, 14

history of Kenya, 10–11, 12–13
holidays, 34–35

houses, 17, 20, 24–25

Indian Ocean, 5, 6

Kikuyu, 14, 16, 20
Kiswahili, 15, 22, 26–27, 32, 34, 42

Lake Turkana, 14
Lake Victoria, 5, 7, 10, 11, 14, 15
languages, 10–11, 14–15, 22, 26–27
Leakey, Louis and Mary, 11

map of Kenya, 4
markets, 20–21, 41
matatus, 18
missionaries, 23, 28
mountains, 6
music, 38–39, 43

Nairobi, 16, 17, 34–35, 39
Nilotic peoples, 11, 14
nomads, 11, 15

people, 10–11, 12–13, 14–15
playtime, 21, 36–37
polygyny, 23, 24
population, 17
Portuguese, 12

religion, 23, 28–29, 35

safari, 8–9
savanna, 6, 7, 8
schools, 21, 26, 32–33
singing, 38–39
sports, 36
stories, 42–43

travel methods, 18–19, 21

weather, 5, 6